A MEMOIR BY

Erika Shelton

Published by 7th Sign Publishing

Book Cover Design by David Boyce
Typesetting by Stewart A. Williams
Copyright ©2021 by Erika Shelton

ISBN: 978-0-578-85151-8
Printed in the United States
Shelton, Erika
Men Over Me

All rights reserved. No part of this book may be reproduced or transmitted in any form or by any means without written permission from the author/and or publisher. The alias names used in this book are given to protect the actual individuals, the author and publisher.

DEDICATION

To everyone who wonders if I'm writing about them, I am.

ACKNOWLEDGMENTS

First, I would like to thank GOD, my LORD and SAVIOUR. Without Him, none of this would be possible. I also thank my loving sons, Ryan and Mikal, for always supporting me in all of my endeavors. Lastly, thanks to my family and friends that have encouraged me to keep going and never give up on my dreams.

CONTENTS

OBIE
-1-

CRAIG
-3-

ANTHONY
-6-

BYRON
-9-

TERRELL
-12-

CHAUCY
-19-

MARQUIS
-34-

FLOYD
-46-

ANTWAN
-56-

ERIKA
-73-

INTRODUCTION - THE ROOT

OBIE

Most little girls grow up adoring and admiring their father: they grow up hoping they will meet a man just like him. They look for someone to protect them, love them unconditionally, while always depending on him to be there. I was born into a two-parent household. I had both my mother and father. My parents separated when I was about five and divorced when I was eleven. Erik, my twin brother, and I would spend every other weekend, spring break, and winter break with my dad. It was never the same as him being in the home.

I never had a close relationship with my dad. I loved my dad but I was never 'Daddy's Little Girl'. I didn't cry for him; I didn't miss him if we skipped a weekend without seeing him. I respected him as my father, but I wouldn't have felt bad if I had disrespected him. It was a strange occasion when he tried to discipline me one day; I didn't listen to him. I told him he had no right to tell me what to do because he didn't raise me. A weekend and holiday dad doesn't mean you've raised me.

While I appreciated him for staying in my life, I knew that he wasn't a part of my life. He never came to our home; he never picked us up or took us to and from school. He didn't even come to my high school graduation. He told us that it was too far to drive. What father tells their children this on one of the most important days of their life?

Many people may think I have daddy issues. I think I love and respect my mother for being there for me when he wasn't. I don't love him any less than my mother. But I know I love my mother more for never missing my tryouts, never missing doctor appointments, and always making sure we had clean clothes and food on the table. My mother spoiled me and my brother: I think because she knew my dad fell short on his responsibilities. I have very high expectations of men … I guess I owe that to my dad. I feel that it is a good thing I have never seen a man go above and beyond. Therefore, I'm waiting for a man to show me.

CHAPTER 1

CRAIG
Crusher

I knew I loved and obsessed over the opposite sex at the tender age of eight. I was in the second grade. We attended St. Matthew's Catholic School. Yes, I was a catholic school girl… doesn't that sound naughty? I had the biggest crush on my classmate, Craig. He was so cute. He had a short afro and pretty white teeth. But, he had a really big head. He was the best looking second grader I had ever seen. We had gym class together. I remembered always starring at him in class. He was a shy kid; one who never really talked to anyone besides my brother and another kid whose name I don't remember. I would ask my brother questions like, "What does he talk about?"… "Who does he like in the class?"… and "What's his favorite sport"?... Just anything to find out more about this 'cutie pie'.

I remember one Saturday night Erik and I were watching *Saturday Night Live* sitting on my mom's bedroom floor. The show was talking about asking a guy out on a date when he doesn't even notice you exist. I had this weird idea to ask Craig something.

I was too young to go out on a date: who would take us… our mothers? I wanted to ask him about something I wanted to experience with only him.

So, I decided I would ask him to go to bed with me. I know it sounds really crazy, but, hey, why not? I wanted to give my 'cookie' to Craig. So, I mustered up the courage to write a note to him: I would give it to him the next time I saw him. I had a plan. I wrote the note; it read: "Craig will you do it with me? Circle yes or no." I know it was straight to the point, as I didn't waste any time. I put the note in my gym bag and waited for Tuesday to pop the question.

Tuesday finally arrived; it was my big day! I was nervous and anxious to see what he said. I was most nervous to see if he would say "yes". Of course, I didn't know anything about 'doing it' then. I mean, I'd seen it on television, but I didn't know. But I had planned to figure it out. I needed to know *how* to give it to him. I would have given the note to my brother, to give to him, but I knew he would open it up and read it. As a result, I knew he will kick my butt. *I can do it*, I told myself. I would then be a woman.

Before gym class I asked one of my friends to call him over so I could give it to him. He came over, smiling, with those pretty white teeth. I said, "Hi", then I gave him the note. I told him not to tell anyone and give it back to me after gym class. He said, "Okay."

I was very scared. I was preparing to become a woman soon. I couldn't concentrate on the exercises we were doing in class. I didn't make eye contact, because I didn't want to seem like I was worried about his answer.

When gym class was over, I went to change back into my uniform. I walked out and went to the cafeteria for lunch. I sat down with my friends. As we were eating, Craig walked up. I immediately got up and stepped to the side, so that no one would hear what we were about to talk about. He smiled and gave me the note. I was so excited… a smile was a good sign.

I waited until I got home to read the note. I wanted to be at home to avoid the chance that anyone would see the note. At home, I ran into the bathroom to be alone. I opened the note with anticipation. My mouth dropped as I looked at the paper. He circled "NO". *What the hell?* I thought. Who says NO to an offer like that? It always worked in the movies.

Men love sex. I mean boys, right? My feelings were crushed. I thought for sure he would say 'Yes'! And to top it all off, he was smiling, with those pretty white teeth. I should have slapped him, right in those 'pearly whites'! I put the note back in my gym bag and threw it on the bed.

My mother was home and making dinner. I started to do my homework when my mother started a load of laundry. I heard the washer going but didn't think anything of it. After a few minutes, my mom yelled, "ERIKA!!!"

She called me the way that only she calls me, which my family made fun of. She said, "Come here, right now"! I get there and saw she had my gym bag and a note in her hand. Right then and there, I knew I was dead.

"What the hell you know about 'doing it'?" she said.

I was speechless. I stood there, frozen.

She said, "Get your ass in there. I'm going to beat your ass, little girl."

I got the beating of my life. I will never forget that day, as long as I live. I competely forgot about 'doing it' with anyone else. I went to school the next day and never looked at Craig the same. He played me. He crushed my 'womanhood'. I felt like boys, young men, grown men, and old men should never turn down sex. Well, I guess I had a hard lesson to learn; believe me. This proved to be so true in my dealings with men in the future. My mother's famous saying was, "A hard head makes a soft bottom".

CHAPTER 2

ANTHONY
Not Child's Play

I had the sweetest, most caring babysitter in the world. Her name was Mrs. Houston. My dad worked with one of her sons at the St. Louis Post Office. He told my dad she babysat kids. My mom was looking for a sitter for us for a couple hours before school and after school. She kept kids of all ages, from newborns to grade school children. She also kept her own grandkids, from time to time.

I loved being there because she treated us like we were her own. Every morning when my mother dropped us off, one of her sons would leave us his left-over breakfast. I know it sounds gross, but we appreciated him for thinking of us. We would always have some eggs, bacon and toast. I looked forward to that. I also looked forward to seeing Mrs. Houston's grandson, Anthony. He was a little older than us. He was really handsome. I really like seeing him. I think he knew I liked him because he would always play with me and tease me.

I was about ten years old, at the time: he was about thirteen, give or take a year or two. He was an athlete. He played basketball;

a game that he was really good at. He became a star player in high school. He was in all the newspapers and on TV. I think he became very successful. I remember one day after school he came over and I was sitting in the kitchen watching cartoons. I don't know how we ended up being the only ones in the kitchen at the time. All the other kids must have been taking a nap.

Mrs. Houston's mother lived upstairs. She would always go upstairs and take her food with her and eat.

•

Anthony came in and sat next to me. He asked what I was watching, and I told him. He then asked if me if he could 'touch me'.

"Touch me how?" I said.

"You know," he replied.

"No … I don't know," I responded.

"I will show you," he said.

"Ok," I replied.

He reached over and put his hand down my pants. He stuck two of his fingers into my vagina. The funny part of this is I know the technical word for it now, but back then my mom referred to it as my "skin". I don't know where she came up with that word, but that was it. Most people say 'pocketbook': that's weird, too.

But anyway, he began to move his fingers around. It didn't hurt; it was okay. I sort of liked it. He did it for about two minutes, not long. It probably would have been longer, but I am certain that he knew he was doing something he had no business doing. He didn't want to get caught, so he stopped.

He never said 'don't tell anyone'… I think he knew I wasn't going to tell … it would be our secret. I always wondered why he picked me to do that to. I wondered if he had done this to anyone else? He was also a kid, therefore, I didn't really blame him for what he did. I think someone may have done it to him.

It didn't damage me or make me feel any differently towards boys or men. I do think it made me love men more. I've always been a very sexual person. I have often wondered if that incident made me that way.

My mother was very open about sex with me and my brother. I remember her buying us books, while always telling us to be very open and honest with her about sex. I appreciate that from my mom, as most parents don't even have that conversation with their kids.

•

My mother always told me to tell her if anyone ever touched me inappropriately. She firmly stated I was supposed to tell her, no matter what the person said they would do or say.

My mother was always so protective of us. I was not allowed to spend the night at any of my friend's houses who had brothers. In addition, my friends were not able to come and spend the night with me, because I had a brother. She didn't play when it came to that. I couldn't sit on any man's lap, even my uncles or cousins. She would've flipped out. I think my mother may have been inappropriately touched when she was little. She has never told me this, but I do feel that something like this must have happened to her. It's okay with me if that was her secret. This too was my secret, until now.

I was not mad at Anthony for what he did. I was angry with myself, because I didn't tell. That could have happened that one time, but it could have also happened all the time to someone that didn't like it or mind like it did. I thought about Anthony for a long time after that happened.

I couldn't wait until I did become of age or an adult to experience it the right way. Instead of making me hate sex or dreading any man touching me again, I wanted that feeling again, more than anything. Did that make me a sex addict or did that just make me want someone to love me? I'd eventually find out that sex isn't love.

CHAPTER 3

BYRON
Freshman vs Senior

When a girl starts high school, she is scared: she doesn't know what to expect. She worries about if she going to be popular: she wonders if she will make the cheerleading team, etc. She also cares about whether or not she will wear the right outfit on her first day. The first couple of weeks went okay. I met some new friends. I started getting used to switching classes. There were some cute guys in my class, but the really cute guys were the upper classmen. I didn't seek out an upper classman, but I didn't shy away from one either.

One day in the hall I walked pass a couple of guys that were seniors. I love dark chocolate men; those that are almost burnt. A particularly dark guy walked up to me and was like, "You are beautiful".

He was not shy at all, and I really like men that tell me the truth. He asked me for my number and the rest was history.

We were inseparable. Whenever and wherever you saw Byron, you saw me. He made me feel like a princess. He gave me everything I wanted. He walked me to all my classes: he didn't care if he was late to his. He would tell everyone that I was going to be his wife. I thought I was the queen of the world. I was a freshman dating a senior… you couldn't tell me shit!

We dated my entire freshman year. He never pressured me to have sex, as we never really talked about it. I know he wanted to, but he was very respectful and didn't push. He asked me to go with him to his senior prom. My mom was so excited that you would have thought I was getting married. It was a big to-do. My mom invited everyone over to see me get ready. It was a big deal. But, that big day almost didn't happen.

The fact that I'm leaving out is that Byron found out a couple days before that I cheated on him. Yeah! I cheated on him with Terrell. (I will talk more about Terrell in the next chapter.) Once Byron found out that I cheated on him with Terrell, he was furious. First off, he found out that I wasn't a virgin, like he thought. He was very disappointed that I gave up my virginity to a guy I had barely known but didn't even consider giving it to him; the guy that everybody loved and thought we would be together forever.

I begged him to forgive me. My mom spent so much money on the prom dress and everything else, so I couldn't tell her that I was not going because I cheated on him. I apologized and apologized until Byron forgave me. He really did love me. We went to the prom and had a really good time. We eventually had sex on the last day of my freshman year. I remember I didn't really like it. It was just okay. It wasn't like I had much to compare it to, but it was very different then it was with Terrell.

Byron was the nice guy that your mother liked. You know… the guy that your mother would let go into your bedroom when she was there and not worry about anything happening. I think I was always attracted to the bad boys: the ones that had a lot of women and weren't available. I know that sounds crazy, but the nice guys just didn't do it for me.

We dated into my sophomore year. I wasn't feeling Byron anymore. I simply knew he liked me a lot and I didn't want to break his heart. I continued to talk to Terrell. We didn't continue to have sex, but I still talked to him every chance I got. Byron and I eventually broke up before Christmas break of that year. I couldn't take it anymore. I think once I had someone to compare the sex to, I wanted the person I thought was best in bed, instead of the one that would treat me right.

Byron wanted it to work out, so he tried for a long time to get back together. But I was too far gone. When I look back at choosing Terrell over Byron, that was the biggest mistake of my life. I was young and this was my first boyfriend. I thought I knew everything. The way a man treats you goes along way. If he treats you like he loves you, then most of the time he does. If he treats you like shit, that means you don't mean shit to him.

I haven't been treated like a queen in a long time. But I have been treated like shit a few times. Byron was the first guy in my life that showed me how a man should treat me. Byron always protected me. He loved to see me smile. He just wanted to make me happy. He was my king. I miss him.

Oh! I forgot to add the fact that Byron wasn't that nice… He did come up to the school to kick Terrell's ass when I started to date him. That was HOT! I almost took him back… (lol). That was the first time I'd seen that 'bad boy' in him.

CHAPTER 4

TERRELL
First Love

This is the guy I mentioned in the last chapter. He was not a nice guy. He was a really bad boy. I had a cooking class with him. He transferred to my school, from another school. He was dark skinned, like I like them. He had bug bubble eyes, and had a greasy curl. He reminded me of one of the guys in the group "Troop". You know the song, "All I Do Is Think of You"? He could have been the lead singer...(lol). He wore tarnished gold rings; one on each hand. He carried a fake Louis Vuitton pouch.

    I knew he was really country, but that was the style back then. He was quiet… he really didn't talk to anyone. We sat at the same table. We would make small talk, from time to time. More and more we started to get to know each other. He never talked about having a girlfriend or that he was interested in anyone, so we just laughed and talk about people in class. He had his clique that he hung out with. It was two of his brothers and couple of friends. They were all thick as thieves.

    I began to like going to my cooking class, because I knew I

would see him. One day he told me that he was talking to one of my homeroom classmates. She was a cute shapely girl. She was nice, but I thought that I was better for him. Did you hear what I said, "I *thought* I was better for him". So that meant I was going to take him away from her. I never considered her feelings or his, for that matter. I wanted to be with him and I just knew it was going to work.

They dated for a while. I would see them in the hall together. He would walk her to her classes and walk her to her bus at the end of the day.

•

The more I would see them together, the more I wanted him. I flirted with him. I kissed him one day after class. I told him I wanted to be with him. I wanted him to break up with her. At first, he didn't want to, but eventually I changed his mind. It got so bad that he was like. "I have to tell her that I'm breaking up with her. I want to be with you". He finally broke up with her and we were not together. I was happy that I had achieved my goal.

We started dating. Then, I became the one he walked to class and was seen with. Well, that didn't last for long. He started to change. He was not the same boyfriend to me that he was to her. I started to feel like he had made a mistake by breaking it off with her to be with me. He stopped walking me to my classes and became more and more distant. He broke it off with me and started seeing the ex again. I felt really stupid. I thought I was doing something by having him break up with her to be with me. What's the saying, "How you get 'em is how you lose them"?

This made me feel like I wasn't good enough for him. Why would he leave someone like me to go back to her? I'm better looking than her… I'm better in bed… These are all the things I'm thinking in my head. I will make him want me more. This was another thing I thought I could accomplish. I have another goal now. Make him want me back and make him regret he ever broke up with me.

It was my mission to make him want me. But all I did was

make him not want me. He continued to date the ex and other girls. I chased him and chased him. The only attention he gave me was to have sex. I was a sophomore in high school. I wasn't that experienced but I wanted to be the best he ever had.

He was the first person that I ever performed oral sex on. At the time, I was sixteen. I knew grown women, in their forties that still hadn't done that. I was growing up way too fast, but I didn't care. He didn't ask me to do it; I wanted to. I thought if I gave it to him really good he would want me. Even after that, I would continue to see him with other girls, talking to them and giving them the attention, I wanted.

It got so bad that I followed him to his gym class. I went to the boy's locker room and asked someone to get him to come outside. He came out and I started to scream and shout at him; asking him why did he have to talk to all these different girls? Why couldn't we get back together… why did he treat me like he didn't care?

He was not trying to hear me. He kept telling me to leave. He threatened to call the security to have me put out. I remember having a lotion bottle in my hand. I then started beating him with it, all upside the head. I was slapping him; just going crazy. I didn't know how to handle my emotions. I couldn't get why he didn't want me. I caused a big scene: the whole gym class came out. The security was called. We got sent to the principal's office and our parents had to be called.

My mother had just had surgery… she was not supposed to leave the house. She was so mad and embarrassed that she had to come up to the school and get me. Terrell's parents had to come up too. My mother was so fed up with me and all the mess over him. She hated him… she saw how I reacted when it came to him. She had asked me before, "What was it about him that made me react so vehemently?"

"Why do you like him so much?" She even asked, "Are you

having oral sex with him?"

WOW! My mother asked me if I was having oral sex because I was going crazy. Both of our parents were furious with us. This resulted in both of us being banned from each other; we were not to see each other or talk to each other... no communication at all.

•

I was so humiliated. The whole school heard about what happened. When I walked down the halls, I would hear people talking and laughing. I heard people saying she is stupid... she is a fatal attraction. I felt like the guys in the school were thinking that I was easy; thinking that I would do anything to be with someone. This thought prevailed because I assumed that Terrell had told people about the things that we experienced.

Terrell was not nice to me for quite some time afterwards. I guess I deserved most of it because he kept telling me he didn't want to be with me, but I just thought I was so fabulous I could change this mind. I also lost girlfriends because of what I did to my friend. Yes, his ex and I were very close, at one point. I didn't care that I wanted her man and wanted to sleep with him, while she was with him.

It took me a long time to get over Terrell and get over that situation. I stopped caring about how I dressed. I would just throw on anything to go to school. I didn't comb my hair half the time. I just didn't care anymore. Terrell was my first love. I lost my drive to do anything. This went on into my junior year in high school.

I finally snapped out of it one day when my loving brother said Erika, "I need to talk to you."

"What happened to my sister?"

He went on to say, "All my friends used to say, 'Man, your sister is so pretty. I wish I could talk to her'."

My twin brother continued; "I don't hear that anymore from my friends. They don't talk about you how they used to. They don't say anything about you."

He said like only a brother could say: "fuck that nigga, Terrell. You don't have to trip off of him anymore. You can do better than that."

•

I then thought to myself, *I must have really been flipping out if my brother cared so much to tell me to 'get over it'.*

I subsequently got better. I snapped out of it. I finished up my junior year and I was excited about being a senior and graduating. The summer came and I was living it up, I was partying every night. I was enjoying my summer. I thought things were changing. I didn't want to be with Terrell anymore, although I still had feelings for him. I know it was crazy, given all the crap I went through, I still wanted him in some way.

We still 'hooked up' a couple times, but I had a better grip on my feelings. I wouldn't go crazy if I didn't talk to him. I was ok. Finally, I could deal with him with no drama. Everything was moving along smoothly, until it happened.

The first day of my senior year in high school finally arrived. The day was good. I walked the halls like I owned the school. Everything was perfect, but something didn't feel right. I had been sick for a couple of days. I thought I had a virus. I asked my friend to go to the doctor with me to see if everything was okay. The doctor examined both me and my friend on that same day. The doctor came out and told me that I was pregnant. He also told my friend she was pregnant. It was unbelievable. We both agreed we wouldn't tell our mothers because they would kill us. We didn't know what we were going to do. I cried all the way home.

I walked in the house with the mindset that I'm going to deal with this… I'm not going to tell her. She will say "Hey, where you been?"

Once I saw her, all of a sudden, I just busted out in tears, saying, "Mama, I'm pregnant! I don't know what to do."

That's just like me to say I'm going to be strong and breakdown as soon as she asks me a question. I don't care… I'm a big baby… I needed my mama.

My mother was freaking out. She said, "You're not going to graduate if you have this baby. You are not going to finish school."

She was thinking my life was going to end. It didn't help that she didn't like Terrell at ALL.

She talked me into having an abortion. I didn't really want one, but I didn't want to disappoint my mother. She told me that if I agreed to have this abortion, she would give me her credit card and I could go shopping. I know it sounds cruel, but she was thinking of anything for me not to have it. So, yes, I aborted a baby over a shopping spree. I told Terrell he really didn't have a care either way. I had the abortion, and I was the best dressed senior that year.

I graduated on time. My mom was happy. That fall, I planned to go to community college and take some courses. Although I said I planned to enroll in and attend community college, things never go as planned.

It was one hot summer night… and, you already know what I'm going to say. I hooked up with Terrell again. I swear I wasn't talking to him. As a matter of fact, I stopped all contact with him. I ran into him at the grocery store. He asked what I was doing that night.

I said, "Nothing".

I should have run out the door when I saw him. I just didn't know when I was going to leave this dog alone. What was my purpose for messing with him?

A couple of weeks later I found out I was pregnant, again. It was exactly a year to date from the last pregnancy. I wasn't giving up my baby this time. I thought to myself, *I could've simply kept the last baby, if I was going to do this stupid shit again.*

I told my mom. Of course, she wasn't happy, but I didn't care. I told Terrell. He didn't think it was his, because I was seeing someone else at the time of our 'hook up'. I knew it was Terrell's child. A woman knows… Besides, the guy I was with had moved out of town.

On May 24, 1991, at 9:37 pm, my love for Terrell ended and my new love Ryan Erik Shelton began.

After nine long months, I delivered a 7lb.,7oz. beautiful baby boy. He changed my life. He made me forget about Terrell. My baby boy made me not want to please any man but him.

Terrell put me through hell: I put myself through unnecessary hell. I was young and thought I was in love. I never knew how much I could have someone until I had him. I now believe in love at first sight. I thank Terrell for my love… that precious baby boy is the nicest thing he has ever done for me.

CHAPTER 5

CHAUCY
Player

I met Chaucy when I was 21. He was a barber in the city. Ryan had just turned one and it was time for his first haircut. I asked around and a friend referred me to this barber shop. I didn't want to go by myself, so I took a girlfriend of mine.

She had heard of the shop. She also wanted to get her haircut. I was thinking about cutting my hair as well. I was tired of my hair: I just wanted something different. We decided to go on a Saturday; the busiest day… not a day you would want to be sitting and waiting to get a haircut.

I had heard about barber shops. I don't think it is anywhere for a woman to be. I think fathers should be taking their sons to a barber shop not women, unless they are personally being serviced. That is just my opinion. But if you have to, as a single parent, then you do what you have to do.

We got to the shop: we walked in. The place was packed. I saw four men cutting hair, along with a lady barber. That was rare back then. We sat down, but we didn't know who we wanted to cut our hair. We were just sort of seeing who we liked. I was looking for the person that most of the people were waiting for. It was a guy that caught my eye. He was a short guy with a bob haircut. He was dressed in some grey sweats and a nice Nike pull over shirt. He had on some fresh Jordan's and a really thin herringbone gold chain. They were popular back then. He was actually cutting a little boy's hair at the time.

I told my friend, "I'm getting ready to ask him to cut Ryan's hair".

So, I walked over and said, "Hi".

"How you doing?" he said.

I asked, "Can you cut my son's hair for me?"

He replied, "Sure."

I said, "It's his first haircut, so I don't know if he is going to cry."

He said, "He will be ok. I gotcha."

The barber continued on to say, "I have another one in front of you, so it will be about 45 minutes before I can get to you."

I said, "Okay." I then added. "I think I want my hair cut off too."

"Yeah! I bet you will look sexy with that cut. I mean you already sexy, but you know…" he replied and smiled.

Well, you know me… I'm weak for a nice-looking man and a cute smile. So, I waited until he was finished. He started with Ryan first. He was really good with him. Ryan started to cry a little, but he sat still and was a big boy. We chatted a little, while he was cutting Ryan's hair. I asked how long he had been cutting hair.

He stated that he had been doing it for about six years already. He seemed to have a nice clientele. The phone was continually ringing; inundated by people calling for him, wanting to get in to get their hair cut.

He finished up with Ryan … now, it was time for me. My hair was a pretty nice length, so he said, "Are you sure you want to cut it all off? It's your last chance."

I said, "Yes. Go ahead."

He cut my hair really short. It was different, but I really liked it.

He said, "Yes! This style fits your face. This style is very becoming on you".

I said, "What? Becoming"?

He replied, "Girl, you look nice."

•

There were other women in the shop that liked my hair, as well as my friend. She let the lady barber cut her hair. It was okay.

My friend stated, "The next time I come, I'm going to let him cut my hair."

I was very satisfied. Therefore, I planned on bringing Ryan back. I was definitely sure that I would come back, for my personal haircuts.

He gave me his business card. I said, "Thank you. I'll see you in two weeks."

When the next two-week time period arrived, I called him at the shop to see if he was there. He was there, so I told him I was on my way.

He said, "Come on up."

On this day, I went without my girlfriend, just me and Ryan. I went on a Thursday. I didn't want to be in there on a Saturday again.

Once I arrived, as soon as I walked in, he said, "I'm almost done." He went on to say, "You look pretty. I see you got your big earrings on and your make up."

Now, you know the next time I went in I had to look cute! He finished up his client and started on Ryan. Again, we chatted. He asked where I lived… if I was seeing anyone. He asked me if I was still in love with my 'baby daddy'. Who asks that?

I also asked him if he was seeing anyone.

He said, "I talk to people, but nothing serious."

Yeah, right! I knew that was a lie when he said that. He was fine.

He asked, "Is it ok if I call you and we can hang out sometime?"

I was looking so stupid. I wasn't used to guys asking me out like that.

I replied, "Yeah. I'll give it to you before I leave."

He finished up with both of our hair. As I went to get my money out of my bag, he said, "You're good."

I asked, "Huh, I'm good?"

He answered, "Yes. You're good. Keep your money."

Again, I was still in shock. I put my money back and give him my number.

He asked, "What are you doing later?

I answered, "Nothing."

He said, "I will give you a call when I get off."

I was cheesing, from ear to ear, when I left. I couldn't wait to leave so I could call my friend and tell her what had just happened.

He didn't call me that day, but he did call the next day. He asked me if I wanted to meet him at this pool hall to watch him play and have some drinks.

I said, "Yes."

I hurried up and got dressed to meet him there. He was about six years older than me, therefore, when I got there, I felt out of place. It was awkward: I felt like I was on a real date. He asked if I wanted anything to drink and eat.

I said "No", like an idiot. You should never go out on a date and not get anything; they might think that you're a cheap date. Years later, I now know better.

I watched him play pool. He was very good. He played for money... he was the man. Everyone knew him there. He drove a gray 4-door Ninety-Eight. He had a little change. Of course, a few women came over and talked to him... nothing really heavy, although I knew he was a lady's man. I could tell. He was very sweet and nice, but one just knew that he was something else.

We had a cool rest of the night. He was a gentleman: he walked me to my car and told me to call him when I made it home. I was so geeked. I was like 'This is my man… wait and see.. we're going to be together.'

•

We chatted and hung out a couple more times. It was cool. I was enjoying his company. There was nothing sexual happening yet. I kissed him a couple of times… he kissed my breasts a bit in the car, but nothing serious yet.

I still continued to go to him to get our hair cut: he still continued to not charge me, financially.

At one specific time, I was there while his daughter was in the shop. He had previously told me about her. I knew how old she was. He also told me about her mother. He dated her mother in high school. At one point, they were engaged, but it didn't work out. I know this sounded sketchy, but I was taking him at his word. The 'baby's mama' later came in. They didn't really talk. She simply picked up her little girl and left. Thus, I concluded, 'They really aren't together'.

Chaucy lived about three minutes from the shop.

He asked me what I was about to do.

I replied with a question, "Why?"

He said, "Because I want you to come see me at my house. I don't have anyone for a couple of hours, so come over."

I replied, "Okay. I will take Ryan to my dad's house."

My dad and his girlfriend at the time, loved keeping Ryan. There was never a need for me to call beforehand, I simply could just drop him off. So, I dropped Ryan off and proceeded on to Chaucy's house.

Chaucy lived with his grandmother and his aunt. It really didn't bother me that he did not have a place to himself, as I knew (assumed) he could afford it.

After I arrived, we sat in the living room. We started to kiss… and one thing led to another. We had sex; it was amazing. He showed me some new tricks. We did the 69, as well as some other numbers that I hadn't even heard of. We hit 100…(lol). The sex was so different from high school sex. It was easy: he did things to me… I did things to him. It was a mutual effort. It wasn't just one person pleasing the other. We both wanted to please each other. I felt like an adult. I felt even more assured that this was my man… we were going to be together.

We never talked about a relationship. We never talked about us being exclusive. It was just easy, with no pressure. I was happy being in this company. I think he felt the same way.

After about six months we were still enjoying each other. Again, I was not thinking I was the only one he was seeing, because we were not together every day, although I was spending a great deal of time with him.

One day he told me he was moving out. He was getting his own place.

I said, "Cool. Where?"

He said, "It is not too far from the shop."

I was really getting excited now; he was getting his own spot. I thought I was going to be there all the time now, with nobody else there. We were really getting ready to be in love.

He moved … I then started to hear less and less from him. I would call the shop, only to be told that "Chaucy didn't come in today, but he will be back in tomorrow."

Damn! What's going on? I thought.

I began to watch my phone, waiting for it to ring… knowing he was off work… wondering why he hadn't called me.

So, you know me… I became a detective: I can find out anything. I knew where his grandma lived. He would always go to check on her after work, or at some time throughout the day. I decided to follow him. I called my friend up to tell what's going on. She and I then began our surveillance operation.

•

We sat at the top of the hill of his grandmother's house and waited until he arrived. He left the barber shop at 6:00 pm. He should have been there no later than 10 minutes after. Like clockwork, he pulled up. He stayed in the house about 10 minutes before he returned to his car. He unknowingly passed us up on the street… we followed him. I remembered him telling me that it wasn't too far from his grandma's house. He went about six blocks from the grandma's and turned on what appeared to be a side street. We kept going so we wouldn't look obvious. It was a dead-end street, so we had to turn around.

He got out of the car and went into the apartment. If I had never been on the street, I wouldn't have known that there were apartments on that street. It was a small building, with four units attached, like a flat. I didn't want to go to the door because I didn't want him to know I was there. So, I called him on his cell phone.

He answered, "Hey. What's up?"

I said, "Nothing. What are you doing?"

He replied, "Nothing. I just got home."

I went on to say, "I haven't heard from you. You've been missing in action."

He said, "Naw, it ain't like that. I've just been busy."

He added, "We're going to get together soon."

I replied, "Yeah, okay. Call me later."

So, then I knew he wasn't living by himself. There was obviously someone staying there with him, or he would've asked me to come over.

I cased out his house a couple more times. I would always see this white Geo Tracker parked on the street. It was a small street, with not a lot of people coming in or going out. So, I figured whoever he lived with drove that car. I thought he must have gotten back with his baby's mama. I had never seen her car, so I didn't know for certain if it was hers. It became my mission to find out what was going on.

I drove by the shop one day and saw that same Tracker. I didn't want to just pop up because we really weren't talking like we used to. I waited for someone to come out and get in the Tracker. It was a very skinny light-skinned girl. She had a mail carrier's uniform on. It wasn't his baby's mama.

She got into the Tracker and went in the direction of the apartment. I followed her. Sure enough, she pulled on that street, parked and went into Chaucy's house (well… her and Chaucy's house).

I was so mad! I wanted to go knock on the door, but decided against it. I called one of my friends; crying and telling her how much I want to f… him up. I wanted to do something to get back. We thought of something so stupid but ingenious at the same time. Nobody would ever think of this.

We called the Ameren power company and had his electricity turned off… We called and gave his name and address and they said his services would be off at the end of that business day. We laughed and laughed: we thought it was so funny. All I could think about was him coming home and trying to flick on the light switch, with nothing happening. I hoped that he had a fridge full or food and they would get home late, to discover that it had all gone bad.

After doing that, I just wanted to ask Chaucy 'what was up with us… what are we doing?' I confronted him about the girl. He told me that they were messing around and they decided to be together. I guess I couldn't get mad because we had never discussed that.

I really didn't want to stop seeing him. I really liked him. I was not in a relationship, but he was. I thought I would just kick it with him until I found someone else. I didn't think it would become a problem. Had he told me that he was with someone, I could have handled it. Instead of just telling him I didn't want to be his 'other woman' or nowadays, his 'side chick'. I just would have gone with the flow. Yeah, right! ...Me go with the flow: I never knew how to do that.

After I found out about the girlfriend, things became quite different. I guess he figured because I knew about her, now everything was cool; meaning he could talk freely about her to me and I wouldn't mind. I would call the shop and ask him what he was doing tonight: he would answer with a comment like, "Oh, do you want to go the movies?" or, "She wants me to stay home tonight." She says, "I'm always out playing pool."

So, I started seeing him less and less. He would squeeze me in on his breaks from work. He would come over for a couple of hours; we would have sex and then he would leave. We didn't hang out at the pool hall anymore. I definitely didn't go to his grandmother's house anymore.

The friend that originally went to the barber shop with me, told me, "I told you he was a dog... you should have never started talking to him."

That was new to me... she had never told me that. I don't know if she thought that we were never around each other, together. She started going to the shop without me. She said he had cut her hair a couple of times when the lady barber wasn't there. Maybe she saw something when she was there, without me, but didn't mention it to me. I just figured she thought he was a dog, like most men are. Well, he was sort of a cheater. I know... I sound stupid. But I liked him. I didn't want to stop seeing him. I just wanted to keep going with the flow.

I finally moved into my first apartment. Prior to this, I temporarily stayed in a shelter for homeless women. I wasn't actually homeless, but one of my friends worked there and she said if I said I was homeless, they could help single parents get apartments.

They would go by your income.

I really jumped on that. That would allow me to see Chaucy more. He could come over and just chill. I thought, now, we can be together more. I actually went to the shelter and literally lived there for about two months. I didn't see Chaucy much during this time. Whenever we talked during the time that I was at the shelter, I had a curfew. I had to be in by 10:00 PM.

Once I received my keys to my new apartment and moved in, I felt like I was really grown up. My rent was $13. I was like I can pay my rent for a whole year! I received food stamps. This enabled me to have a fridge full of food. I had it made. It seemed as if I had more money being unemployed than I did when I was working.

My mom was so happy. The apartment was really nice. She bought Ryan an entire bedroom set, including a TV, along with all the decorations. My aunt decorated my bedroom and my dad bought me my bedroom mattress. I already had a bedroom set. My thoughts immediately went to 'when Chaucy comes over, he is going to love it. He is going to leave her and want to move in with me.'

As you already know, my plans never work out the way I think they will.

Chaucy came over… he said, "This is nice. You've got it looking good."

We christened every room in the apartment; even the hallway leading to the stairs in my apartment. It was always good with him.

For the next couple of months, we did see each other a little more. He did try to come over more when he could get away. He would call and say, "What are you cooking?"

I really didn't know how to cook, but I would put something together for him. He would come over and sometimes fall asleep. This would cause me to think, "Yep, he loves it here: he doesn't want to leave me."

Whenever she would call his cell phone, I would want to pick it up so badly and tell her, "He is with me now."

But he would always get up and go home. He would never spend the whole night. I was getting frustrated that he wasn't saying 'I want to be with you… I will leave her.' I started to feel like he was never going to leave her. My first thought was I was going to call her to tell her, but that thought went out of my head. I was very stressed out. I was constantly having to think of something I could and should do to make the situation better. I just ended up making it worse. I could never just let things be.

I was so busy stressing that I was not really paying attention to what was happening to my body. My breasts were becoming really sore. I was waking up nauseous… not eating enough. I had no idea that I could be pregnant. I told my girlfriend that I may be pregnant. I didn't think about having another child. I didn't think about how Chaucy would react when he found out if this was the case.

I bought a pregnancy test. I got home and peed on the stick… sure enough, the stick turned blue. I was pregnant. I called my friend and we were both in shock. Here I was pregnant. Not only pregnant with my second child and unmarried, but pregnant by a guy that had a live-in girlfriend. I didn't know what I wanted to do or was going to do.

I called Chaucy and told him I had something to tell him. I told him that he needed to come over. I was so nervous; I didn't know how to start… I didn't know what to say.

He came over; looking fine as usual. We talked for a bit and then started kissing. Of course, we ended up having sex. I thought to myself, "I want to get it in one last time before I tell him, because he might not want to see me anymore."

After we finished having sex, we were just chillin' and watching TV. I just came out and said it.

I said, "Chaucy, I'm pregnant."

He didn't say anything for a minute. Then he said, "What?" He went on to say, "I don't want any more children."

He had a girl with his 'baby mama' and a boy with another girl, although he said he was not really sure if the boy was his.

I said, "Well, I'm pregnant, so what are we going to do?"

He said, "You can do what you want to do, but I'm telling you, I don't want any more children."

I got mad and told him it was time for him to go. I didn't know how me telling him I was pregnant was going to go, but I didn't think he would say that. He left. I called my friend and told her what he said.

She angrily screamed, "I told you he wasn't shit!"

I was furious. I decided I was going to keep the baby. I told my mom. She wasn't happy. She commented with a question, "Are you just going to be on welfare and just keep having babies?"

I didn't like that, but I wasn't having another abortion. I started making my doctor's appointments and began taking my vitamins. I still continued to talk to Chaucy, even though he had begun to be mean to me. He would ask how I was feeling and how I was doing, but he stopped coming over. I would ask him to come over, but he would say, "I want to, but I think that's not a good idea."

I still continued to take Ryan to his barber shop to get his haircut. I was there one day waiting for him to cut his hair and his girlfriend came in. She had on her postal uniform. She came in and gave him a kiss. I just sat there. No one in the shop knew Chaucy and I had been 'messing around'.

Chaucy looked somewhat nervous, but he played it cool. She went over and talked to the lady barber. She was talking about work and said that she was on her way to her doctor's appointment.

The barber lady said, "Yeah. Chaucy told me that y'all were expecting."

She happily replied, "Yes!"

The lady barber asked, "When are you due?"

She said, "The beginning of July."

Damn! My due date was July 19th. Ain't that some shit? I was boiling inside. I looked at Chaucy and he had his head down the whole time. I wanted to fuck him up. He told me that he didn't want any more kids, but this bitch was pregnant.

You mean you don't want any by me, right! I thought.

My feelings were so hurt. He had a couple of customers waiting before us, so I just said, "Hey, I will just come back later, when you're not so busy," and I left.

I went to my mother's house and told her what Chaucy had said. She said, "Erika, you knew he had a girlfriend. Also, he told you he didn't want any kids. You know if you keep this baby you will be basically raising him by yourself."

She didn't comfort me. She didn't say, "Baby, it's going to be alright." She told me the truth. I didn't want to hear that.

You know it was on, now. I called one of my friends that didn't care about doing dirty, mean things. (This was a different friend than the one who helped me turn off his electricity…) Together, we decided that we wanted to do something that would cost him; something that would have to come out of his pockets. We went to the store and bought some PINK spray paint. We waited until about 12:30 AM. We wanted to make sure that he and his woman were in for the night. We spray painted his Ninety-Eight. We painted, "Chaucy ain't shit" all over the hood and doors. We fucked it up. That felt really good.

He knew I had something to do with it. My 'friend' and I thought we had really done something. We rode around the next day to see if his car was still sprayed. He had it parked in the front of the shop. The car was clean, paint-free and shining. The white-walled tires were on point. We were like, "What the hell happened to the paint?"

Later on, I found out we had bought the spray paint that

washed off... it wasn't the permanent paint. I should've known something was off when he wasn't calling or coming to kick my ass. I finally realized that nothing was changing: he wasn't going to leave her. He wasn't going to be a part of my baby's life. The lesson that I learned from this was, 'When someone tells you something, listen to them. Don't hear what you want to hear, hear exactly what they are saying.'

I thought he really cared about me because he was cheating on this girlfriend that I knew he loved. So, I thought he must love me too. I couldn't believe I was pregnant with his child and his girlfriend was too, at the same time! Here I was pregnant with no fathers for both of my children. Nonetheless, I was determined that I would be a great mother, despite the fact that I was destined to be a single parent.

I never went back to the barber shop after that day. I got bigger and bigger as my pregnancy progressed. I would still talk to Chaucy, every now and then, but he was basically out of my life. I never asked him for anything. I told him when the baby was coming and hoped he would be there for his birth. I hoped he would change his mind.

•

The day came for my baby to be born. On July 22, 1994, I welcomed Mikal De'Andre Cole into this world. He weighed in at 6 lbs., 12 oz. When I look back on it, I should have given him my last name to keep our legacy going. Ryan has our family name. But once again, I thought I was in love. There was still a little part of me that thought it would make Chaucy have a change of heart.

Mikal was so cute; he looked just like Chaucy. My friend called Chaucy for me when I was in labor, but he never showed. By this time, I am wholly into the realization that I now have two beautiful boys to raise... I don't have time to be 'tripping' over any man. I now had two little men to care for.

To assure myself that I didn't make this same mistake again,

I asked my doctor to tie my tubes. I was 23 years old. He advised me that that wasn't a good idea, considering my age at the time. He told me that I could meet someone that I wanted to be with and marry. I told him that I didn't care. I was a 23-year-old unwed mother: I didn't want to repeat this situation anymore.

I knew damn sure I was going to keep having sex. So, the doctor finally agreed. He tied, clipped and burned my tubes. Now, there is not a chance that this would ever happen again. Given my track record with men, it was okay with me. I was just fine being by myself.

Chaucy never came around. I was doing it all by myself, but it was good. I lost track of him for a very long time. I eventually did run into him in the grocery store when Mikal was about five years old. Mikal was with me at the time. He said he wanted to start seeing him, so we exchanged numbers, but he never called. It was okay. I was over that situation by that point.

Oh! I also found out about two years after Mikal was born that my friend that originally went to the barber shop with me called and told me that she slept with Chaucy while we were messing around. Yes! My friend that I thought I was cool with, was sleeping with my baby's daddy; called me and told me. We had a 'falling out' about something stupid… I don't remember. But I guess she called herself getting back at me. Wow! That was deep. Before she got off the phone she said, "See, I told you he was a dog and wasn't shit!"

CHAPTER 6

MARQUIS
Step Daddy

I met Marquis when I was getting off work. During this time, I had a seasonal position at a bank. I ran across the street to get something to eat. There was a fish place my coworkers would go to for lunch. They said it was pretty good. I went in and looked at the menu. There was so much to choose from. I couldn't decide what I wanted, so I asked the guy what was good.

He said, "Everything." But he was really rude with it.

I asked, "How much is your tripe sandwich?"

He coldly replied, "Lady, it's on the menu. I have a lot of orders I need to get out and my phone is ringing. If you don't know what you want, then just let me know when you do."

I was thinking to myself, *"He is a dick."*

I decided to get the tripe sandwich. I ordered my food and waited for it to be prepared. My brother was waiting for me outside in the car. When I got in I told him there was a rude ass dude in there taking orders.

He said, "I know this dude who works in there named Marquis."

I said, "Well, I don't know what his name was. He didn't have on a name tag, but he was real nasty."

When I got home, I opened my sandwich; it was horrible. It had no hot sauce and no pickles. It was just plain and nasty. So, I called the number on my receipt to complain. When the phone rang, a guy answered. I explained to him that I had just left, having ordered a sandwich and it was all wrong. The guy apologized and told me to come back in and he would give me my money back or I could get something else.

•

The next day I want to go to that same place for lunch, but I was really busy. Thus, I decided to go when I got off. I walked in and asked for the manager. It was the same guy standing in the window from the day before.

He said, "I'm the manager."

I said, You're the manager!"

He answered, "Yeah."

I said, "Well, do you remember I was in here yesterday?"

He said, "No, I don't remember."

"Well, you messed up my order. I called and spoke to someone and they said you would refund my money or give me something else."

He replied, "I don't know who would tell you that. I don't give refunds. All my food is good. I make it myself."

I snapped back, "Well, that damn tripe sandwich wasn't good!"

We kept going back and forth. I couldn't believe he was a manager talking like that to me.

I said, "Dude, I want my money back."

He said, "Okay. I will give you your money back. Can I have your number?"

I shouted, "Hell no! You are so rude. I don't know how you are still in business!"

My brother was outside waiting in the car. He was wondering why it was taking so long. He finally came in.

Erik said, "What's up, Marquis man?"

The guy behind the counter replied, "What's up, Erik?"

I was in shock. I said, "Is this your friend you were talking about?"

My brother said, "Hey, man. This is my twin sister; the one I used to talk about."

"Oh yeah." Marquis then said, "Yeah! She's been in here giving me a hard time. I asked her for her number, but I guess she doesn't like me."

I said, "You are rude as hell." I got my food and we left.

A couple of days later he showed up at the bank I worked at to get change for the restaurant. I wasn't a teller; I was collecting payments for personal property taxes. He finished with one of the tellers and came over to my window. He asked how I was doing and if I was still not going to give him my number.

I said, "I don't know."

He grabbed one of the pens on the counter and wrote his number down. He said, "Call me, please."

Marquis was light-skinned, with the prettiest hazel eyes. You know I'm not into light-skinned guys. But come to think of it, all the dark-skinned guys were no good. He had sexy lips and he stood about six feet tall. I loved that. Only short men approached me. I love tall men. I like the fact that when you lie to them, you don't have to look them dead in their face.

He wasn't bad on the eyes, but I didn't care. He worked at a fish place and he smelled like it. I decided I would call him and see what he was talking about.

When I called him, we had good conversation. He told me he had a son. He also told me that he was a little sad because his baby's mama moved to Atlanta and took the child with her. He told me that she was really silly and crazy.

I thought to myself, *"Oh God, I don't want to deal with that."*

But he was nice. He always wanted to see me. If it was just for five minutes out of the day, he always wanted to spend time with me. He would come over on his breaks and talk to me, or I would go over to the restaurant and talk to him. I loved the attention he was giving me. He would ask me to come over to his house. I wasn't really comfortable with that. He wasn't trying to get in my pants, he just said he didn't want me to be away from him.

We would talk on the phone all night. We would laugh and just talk. It felt really good to find someone that was into me. He kept asking me to spend the night, but I didn't want to take my kids over there. I really didn't know much about him, insofar as the type of people he hung around with. I was living back with my mother, at the time. So, I told her I was going to stay the night with my friend.

She asked, "What friend?"

I said, "Marquis."

She had heard me talk about him. She said, "Oh! He has his own place?"

I said, "Yes."

"You can't take Ryan with you. Take the baby."

Mikal was about eight months old at the time. So, Mikal and I packed up and went to Marquis' house. Marquis lived on the west side of St Louis. Anyone that knew about the west side knew it was not a good area to live. He lived on Hamilton. We got there and knocked on the door. Marquis was so excited because I was there. It was a two-family flat. It was old and really run down.

When you walked in you entered the living room and went through another bedroom. Marquis' room was in the back. He lived there with his friend Bud, but they called themselves cousins. Marquis had a heater on the floor in his room, as it was cold in the house. Like I've said, it wasn't the best apartment, but I was glad to be there with him.

Marquis liked playing and bonding with Mikal. He would take him in the room with him and Bud. They would play games and watch TV. They would leave me in the room as if I weren't even there. We were there every night. I would get off of work and go home. I would pack Mikal's and my bags and we would be headed to Marquis' house.

•

I don't know why my mother never wanted me to take Ryan. I guess because he was older and she really didn't want him to be just meeting anyone I don't know. I think she was getting jealous that I was spending all my time with Marquis.

She once said, "Well, maybe he doesn't want you there every night. You can stay at home sometime."

I said, "Mama, that's my boyfriend. I believe he wants me there every night."

I started trying to make the place 'girly'. I went out and bought shower curtains and rugs for the bedroom, to make it look better. I bought a new comforter set for the bed. I bought pictures for the walls. It was really starting to look nice.

One night Marquis lit the fireplace and we slept in the living room, on the floor. It was Marquis, Ryan, Mikal and me. It was so nice… we were a little family. It felt good to finally have a man all to myself; someone to call my boyfriend. Someone that liked me as much or even more than I liked him. I think it is always good for the guy to like you just a little more then you like him. I think it cuts out just a little less heartache.

Marquis and I were in love. We always wanted to be with each other. He was so loving and caring. He always told me he loved me. He would say things you would hear in movies. He could make me cry, just by telling me his feelings. He was the first guy that I had an organism with. I thought I had one before, but I didn't. It was a very different feeling than what I thought it was. It was a feeling I always wanted to feel when I was having sex. I don't know if it is because we were really in love and really into each other, but it was great. Marquis used to call me "Ladybug". This was his pet name for me.

I went out and got a tattoo of 3 lady bugs with his initials, walking to my cookie. Most men don't even notice it when they are down there. After five months of being together, we moved into our own apartment. I know that was really fast, but I was very excited. My mom was even loving Marquis. If my mama liked you, you were in. Marquis was really good to my kids, especially Mikal.

Mikal started calling Marquis 'daddy'. I know that's a lot, but he was always around. Marquis didn't mind. He took care of all of us. He cooked dinner, he washed clothes, he cleaned up everything. He even potty-trained Mikal. It was so cute when he went to the bathroom, he took Mikal. He looked so cute showing him how to point his little pecker into the toilet. He was a good daddy and an awesome boyfriend. He would get sad sometimes when he would think about his son a lot.

Sometimes I would come in the room and he would be just staring at his picture. His baby's mama was really putting him through it. He would do anything for his son. He would send him clothes and send her money. But, if it wasn't what she wanted she did not appreciate it. I know how much he wanted to be in his son's life. If he was breaking his back to provide for me and my kids, he damn sure would have done it for his own. I never stopped or hindered him from being a part of his life. She was very silly. We had words a couple of times on the phone when she would call the house. I know she didn't like the fact that Marquis was raising some other woman's kids. I think she still wanted him back.

Our relationship was going well: it was moving at a steady pace. The kids were getting older and I felt like it was time to start planning a future. A real future: a couple of my friends had gotten married and started buying homes. I felt we needed to stop playing house and start making our relationship a real committed one. We talked about getting married. Marquis was all for it. He was willing to do anything that made me happy. I wanted him to get another job, a better job. He was so smart, and he could do anything. He was a very hard worker.

I wanted him to go back to school and do anything just to better his career. He seemed like he was content just working at the restaurant. It was his close friend's business. But his friend was never there. Marquis basically ran the place. He would only show up when it was a big catering event that Marquis worked his butt off to host and he would take all the credit. I didn't really care for him because I felt he was taking advantage of him. But you can't tell men anything about their friends; they have to learn for themselves.

We started to argue about his job and him not being motivated to do anything else. If anybody knows me, they know that I have a really foul mouth. So, I started calling him really bad names. Sometimes I would say…

"You're acting like a bitch…",

"You're stupid …"

"You just let people run over your dumb ass."

"You ain't going to be shit!"

… Just really hurtful things. I didn't really mean them; I just didn't know how to get through to him to make him change or understand what I was saying. When I get mad, I see RED and I don't think about the things I say until after I have said them. Then, it's too late.

It was really getting bad. I started putting him out. It was both of our apartment, but Marquis had some warrants and he couldn't get on the lease. Therefore, the apartment was just in my name, so I felt like I had that power over him. We discussed that I would never put him out. But I would get so mad and it would just come out. The first time I put him out, he was only gone for about three hours. He went over to his great grandmother's house, at the time. She was still living then. She raised Marquis: he loved her to death. We talked about it and he came back.

•

We were good again for about six months and I said get out again. This time he was really mad. "You told me that you would never do this and now this is the second time," he said.

He had just done the grocery shopping a few days before. He also had just bought me the bathroom set I wanted. I wasn't at home when I told him to get out. When I arrived home, he had taken all the groceries out of the fridge. There was nothing left. He also took the bathroom set he just bought. He took the shower curtains, the rugs, the face towels, toothbrush holder; everything. I guess he thought *'If I've got to go, I'm taking this shit that I just bought with me.'* That was pretty childish to me but he did what he needed to do. This time he was gone for about two weeks.

We talked on the phone and he eventually came back. By this time, we weren't getting along. We were just putting up with each other. I didn't want to break up with him; I just wanted him to do more. He tried to make me happy. He proposed to me that Christmas. It was nice. I had a cute little diamond. It was cool: it satisfied me a little bit. But he was still working that crappy job.

I started liking this guy on my job. He was really sexy. He reminded me of Denzel Washington. We would talk most of the day at work. Marquis would see me talking to him when he picked me up from work. Marquis didn't have a car at the time. He was driving mine, which was also another thing that was getting on my nerves. It's like everything I didn't care about at first now started to matter.

Marquis asked who the guy was that I was talking to at work. I just said we work together: he has a girlfriend. It wasn't long after that time that I started having sex with the guy. I would tell Marquis I was working late and that I would call him when I was ready to be picked up. I would leave with the guy, go to his house and have sex. Afterwards, he would drop me off at the job so Marquis could pick me up.

I felt really guilty because Marquis would be home with the kids; making dinner, doing homework, playing games and bonding with kids that were not even his own kids. He would be babysitting while I was having sex with another dude. But there were other times that I didn't feel bad. I felt he should have been doing more, like getting another job. So, sometimes I didn't care. Here I am. I have finally gotten a decent boyfriend; one that is all mine…one who loves me and my kids to death, and I'm cheating on him.

I continued to cheat on him and wasn't really having sex with Marquis anymore. You know how it is; when someone else is in the picture, everything the one you have at home does begins to get on your nerves.

If he said, "Good morning, Baby", I would say, "What?" Just snapping at him. It wasn't good.

We got into this big fight again over something stupid. So, I said those famous two words again.

I shouted, "GET OUT!"

By this time, he was fed up with my shit.

He said, "Oh, yeah. If I leave this time I'm not coming back. You will never be able to talk me into coming back."

I said, "I don't give a fuck! Leave!"

You know I had that side piece, so I said, "I'm good."

I wasn't thinking about how I was going to have to pay all the bills and do everything on my own. I really didn't want to go back to that lifestyle. It wasn't fun doing it all alone. But I was not thinking about anyone but myself. I wasn't thinking about what it would do to my kids. Especially Mikal. He worshipped Marquis. He followed him around everywhere: he loved him.

Marquis left and we didn't talk for about a month. He would call and talk to Mikal and Ryan, but he wouldn't talk to me. He ended up getting into with his friend and quit. He had to find another job. He had become friends with one of my coworker's brothers, who hooked him up with a job at a lawyer's office. He would go out and serve subpoenas to people. I was happy for him. Finally, he got a real job.

I started to miss him being there. I was still seeing the other guy, but you know that was just for the sex. The other guy wasn't trying to be with me. I asked Marquis to come back and he said 'no'. I thought he would come around. I waited a little longer, then I asked again, "Please come back."

He said, "No. I'm not coming back."

He wasn't telling me he loved me on the phone anymore. He just wasn't the same. I still didn't think he was seeing anyone. I kept thinking, 'I got him… he loves me. He doesn't want anybody else. He is just trying to play hard to get.'

My coworker told me that her brother hooked him up with this girl at the job.

She went on to say, "She is a freak. She fucks all the guys on the job. He even had sex with her."

I said, "Oh, yeah. He is messing with this bitch?"

She answered, "Yeah! Ask him and see what he says."

She added, "Oh, and she is a WHITE BITCH."

My heart fell out of my chest … A WHITE BITCH! That figures.

Why do black men feel that they have to mess with a white chick? I'm not racist at all, but there are some good sisters out here. Why do they have to go there? I hear the men say they don't talk back. They say that they 'give good head'. That's bullshit! Black women will stand on their damn head and suck a dick. They will do anything for a black man, if not more than a white chick. Black men are beautiful things. They always have been and always will be.

Of course, when I asked him, he lied. He said he didn't like her because she wasn't his type. Yeah, right!. Even though I was fucking with this other dude, it didn't matter. You don't fuck with another bitch. That's breaking the code. I couldn't trust him anymore, but I still wanted him back. I now knew I wanted him back, simply because he was messing with the white chick. We went back and forth about him coming back. While he was eventually willing to come back, he didn't want to get put out again.

Just as he was deciding if he wanted to come back, he called and told me something that broke my heart in a million pieces. He told me she was pregnant.

I cussed him out. I said, "Of all the n….s at the job that fucked this bitch, you had to be a dumbass and not wear a condom."

I was so mad and hurt. He told me that he loved me and he wanted us to work, but it was too much shit that had happened. He told me he didn't love her; he just wanted to be there for his baby. He wanted to be in the household with his child and to know how that felt. He wanted to raise her with both parents. I knew he wanted that… he missed his son so much.

He wanted to be a great father and do right by his own kids. I knew he loved my kids, but it wasn't the same. I think if he would have stayed, he would have ended up resenting me and my kids because he didn't try to be there for his own. Marquis never came back. We still talked and he still came by to see Ryan and Mikal. But after about six months, he just stopped coming around. He told me it was hard to see them and me; he missed us very much, but he had to do this for this child.

•

I was hurt for a long time. I felt that he abandoned us. I felt like he never really loved my kids. How could he just leave? I know my cussing him out and saying he 'wouldn't ever be shit' took a toll on him. No man wants to be cussed out and downgraded by the woman that's supposed to love him. We still kept in contact over the years. He went back to school.

He is now a successful machinist, making good money. And he is still with the white girl that he said he didn't like. His daughter is now in college. I'm happy for him… no hard feelings. He had to do what was best for his child.

I lost the man of my dreams; the man that made me feel so special. The one that would have done anything for me. I fucked that up trying to be his boss and not his partner. I have learned now you have to let a man be a man. Let him make his own decisions, and it will happen at the right time. You can't force him to do anything he isn't ready to do. It will all come around in time. You just have to be patient….

"It always seems like there is just one person to love, until you find someone else."

CHAPTER 7

FLOYD
He Got a Ring on It

Floyd was different from all the other guys I've dated. He was light skinned and he didn't have pretty teeth. He was tall and very skinny. His legs were so boney. It wasn't sexy at all, but he was nice. He really stood out from all the other guys. He changed my life in a big way. He was MARRIED. I know you're thinking, *"Why is she involved with a MARRIED man?"* Well, I tried the love thing. I thought I found the man of my dreams and that shit didn't work. So hey, let's try this out.

    I didn't intend on messing with a married man. It just happened. I met Floyd at the barbershop. I used to take Ryan and Mikal to this guy a couple times when they were little. He opened up a shop in his home. I liked that I didn't have to worry about a crowded shop. He only took people he knew and referrals. I saw Floyd, a regular customer, a couple of times but never really had a romantic interest in him. Again, he wasn't my type.

    He was always talking about basketball. He coached basketball to small boys. He was very passionate about that. We both would arrive at the shop around 7:00 am. I hated the barber shop, so I wanted to be there as early as possible, so I could get out quickly. He would always give a nice "Hello" greeting. He was very polite. I loved his voice; it was very assuring, as he spoke with confidence. His tone wasn't arrogant; rather it was very sexy, in my opinion.

Floyd sometimes brought his daughter with him, to the barber shop. She was a daddy's girl. I thought it was sweet. He would give her anything she wanted. I think what most attracted me to him that he was very kind and loving. I would watch him with his kind, caring interactions with his daughter. I could tell that he would be a good guy to be with. He would be very supportive; always there for you. That was something I needed at that time.

He would talk to all the kids in the shop, even Ryan and Mikal. He would ask them about their favorite sports. He would ask them if they liked basketball. I think he wanted to recruit them for his team.

We started talking every Saturday morning. I would look forward to seeing him on Saturdays. I started asking questions about basketball, just to try to strike up a conversation. He was a talker, so he enjoyed running his mouth. His wife would call sometimes. I suspected it was her because he would always step out and answer the phone. Believe it or not, he was very respectful. Whenever she would call, I would feel somewhat angry. My thoughts were like, *"Damn. Why is she disturbing us?"*

We continued to 'bump' into each other at the barbershop. I was intentionally bumping into him. One Saturday we both arrived at the same time. He said the boys could go first; he opted to wait. He said he was going to get a cup of coffee. He asked if anyone needed anything? I thought that was my chance… I think he was waiting for me to say, "Yes. Can I ride with you?"

I did just that. We went to get coffee. It was sort of awkward, but I was excited. We got the coffee and pulled back up at the house. We didn't get out of the car right away: we just keep talking. I didn't want to leave him. I asked him what his plans were for the day. He answered by saying that he had a basketball game and a couple of errands to run.

I said, "Okay. Well, it was nice talking to you."

He replied, "It doesn't have to end. You can give me your number and I can call you later."

I was shocked that he actually asked for my phone number… it seemed as though he was never going to ask.

I gave him my number and said just give me a call when you have time. I didn't think he was really going to use it. But to my surprise, he called as soon as he left the barbershop. I loved his voice, as it was so comforting. I felt like a high school girl around him.

We talked all the time. He called me every morning on his way to work. We talked all throughout the day. We talked on his way home from work. He would make every effort to talk to me. He would make up excuses to run to the store so he could call me. I loved that attention. My attraction to him was a mental thing.

We finally had sex after about two months. I invited him over one day. I think it was a holiday. I remember that the kids were out of school but they were not at home. I remembered it being really awkward. We kissed for a while. He was a great kisser. I was ready to get it on. I think he was a little scared. I could tell he really loved his wife. I don't think he really wanted to jeopardize their relationship. We knew that it would happen soon…meaning that it was the next step, since we had already kissed.

He had protection. I appreciated that. That was a sign of some respect. The sex turned out to be just okay; it wasn't nothing to brag about. He was actually so skinny that his body laying on me was somewhat painful. I'm used to a thicker man.

Even though the sex wasn't the best, I was so attracted to his demeanor, his voice and his intelligence. The sex didn't matter.

MEN OVER ME

He had my mind, as I was so into him. I got used to talking to him; used to seeing him at least once a week. I always saw him on Saturday mornings. The kids didn't get their hair cut every Saturday, but he did. So, I made sure I was there on Saturdays, to see him.

•

I remember on 9/11 when the two planes crashed into the Twin Towers, we were on the phone talking. Everybody was in a panic. My job let us off early. He talked to me all the way home. He waited on the phone with me until I got gas. All the gas stations were packed. Everybody was afraid that we would run out of gas. He was so caring. I don't think he even checked on his wife. He was always there for me. He didn't give me money or pay my bills, but he did support me in every way. I felt a connection with him. I felt like we were really in a relationship.

We talked about my hopes and dreams; my decisions in life. How I wanted to marry a man like him… just not a cheater (lol). He knew when I was upset. He knew when I had something on my mind. He knew everything about me. He really understood me. I felt like I should have been his wife.

I began to wonder why he was so into me and not like that with his wife. Our connection was so strong, I just knew that his wife must have really been in love with this man. I often wondered why he decided to cheat with me? What made me so special? Why was he not so attentive to her? It didn't matter. I wanted him and I no longer cared about the fact that he was married. I wanted him all to myself. I didn't want to share him with her anymore.

I thought about him day and night. If he didn't call at the exact time he should've called, I would be so mad. I would pick a fight with him. I would start questioning him… asking what was he doing? Why did it take so long for him to call me? I even start asking about his wife.

They were general questions like; where she worked… and how long they been together. I asked everything… and like a dummy, he told me. Men really don't think about what they tell you. They tell you all their business, not thinking it could be held against them at any moment.

One morning he didn't call on his way to work. I was furious. I don't know why, but when I get mad, I do dumb shit. I'm not thinking that maybe he simply didn't have time; or possibly he was talking to his daughter, etc. I was just mad he didn't call when he was supposed to. When he finally called, I was silent for a bit.

He asked if I was okay. He even said he was busy that morning and wasn't able to call.

I did not respond with anything like, "Okay, baby. That's fine."

I'm a little spoiled and want things to go my way. Therefore, I really didn't care what he was talking about. I was mad. We went back and forth, a couple of times. We never really argued, but I was picking this fight. I told him,

"You must have been fucking her last night, so you were too tired to call." I also said, "Aww, that's cute! You are all in love now… that's why you didn't call."

At first, he was like, "Naw. It ain't like that, baby. I was just busy."

I kept going and going. Then he started getting angry. He rarely yelled or cursed.

He said, "Erika, if I want to fuck my wife, I can. And if I didn't call you because I was busy, like I said. And another thing… I don't have any obligations to you. If I don't want to, I just won't call. Deal with it!"

My heart dropped. I was in shock. He never spoke to me that way.

I said, "Fuck you. I will tell your wife." I meant that, as I said it with no hesitation.

He said, "Yeah, right! You will not tell my wife."

I guess he thought I was joking, or that he could psych me out.

So, I said, "Yes! I will get off the phone and call her and tell her everything."

Little did he know that when he told me where she worked, I investigated further and found out exactly where she worked. Like I said, be careful what you tell somebody because they will surely hold it against you.

He said, "Do what you have to do."

I said, "Okay," and hung up.

Once I hung up, I didn't hesitate for even two seconds. I immediately called her job and asked to speak to her. She answered the phone.

I said, "Hi! You don't know me, but I have been messing with your husband for months."

She said, "Oh! Okay!" And she hung up the phone.

It felt so good. I didn't think about her feelings or I just ruined someone marriage. I always did things to people when I got mad or didn't get my way and didn't care at the time that I was doing it. I never worried about how it would affect all parties involved. I told a friend that I worked with about what I had just done. She couldn't believe it.

The coworker/friend said, "Erika, she didn't have anything to do with that." She also said it was wrong.

I still didn't care, at that moment. I was just trying to hurt Floyd. I was thinking after I told her she would call him yelling and screaming and then he would be calling me.

Wrong! That didn't happen. He didn't call me at all. I thought maybe she would convince him to call me back and then we would all be on the phone arguing. I loved drama, so I was ready.

But nothing happened. For two whole days, I didn't hear anything. I called him at work and they said he was off for the rest of the week.

"*Oh, shit!... What's going on?*" I thought.

I was wondering if he had moved out... did they break up... did she kill him? I was going crazy. I don't know why I thought that once she found out, he was going to come crawling to me... But I did.

I got up enough nerve to call his cell phone. It went straight to voicemail. I kept calling every hour, no answer. I finally stopped calling and figured he wasn't going to call. I don't blame him. He should never want to talk to me.

After about a week, he called me at work. I didn't know what to say, but was glad he called. I apologized a hundred times for what I did and begged him to forgive me.

He said he forgave me, but we couldn't see each other anymore. He said he wanted to work things out with his wife. I didn't understand it, but I could accept it. I asked if we could still talk on the phone sometimes.

He said, "Yeah, that would be cool."

We started talking again, normally, in about two days. It was if I had never told his wife. He didn't come over my house. I guess he couldn't really get away like before, but we would still talk all the time. I wanted to touch him and kiss him and feel his body close to mine. I would do anything to be in his company.

He stopped coming to the shop on Saturdays so he wouldn't run into me. I didn't understand why he didn't want to see me, but he continued to talk to me like before. I guess he couldn't stand to be around me either, because he would give in or I he possibly thought that I couldn't handle it. He told me where he worked but I didn't really know how to get there. He told me he was working overtime and he had to get up really early to go in. I decided I would follow him to work, so I could see him.

Oh, yes... I also knew where he stayed. Yep, like a dummy, he told me what street he lived on. He didn't give me the address, but that was easy: I only had to look for his car.

•

I got up about 4:30 AM and drove to his house. I parked down the street and waited until he came out. He came out about 5:10 AM. He got into the car and drove off shortly thereafter. I followed behind him. I followed him all the way to work. I saw him pull in the garage and go into the building. I was so happy I got to see him. I didn't want to approach him because I didn't know what he would say or do. He would really think that I was a lunatic. I did that for a week straight, just to see him. I was losing control.

We kept talking as usual, but things weren't the same. He wasn't so attentive anymore. He didn't seem to be 'into me' anymore. I had broken a bond and connection that we shared. I tended to do that with the people I cared about. It's like I have to take over and prove who I am. I have to show them what I'm capable of. I pretend like I don't give a fuck about them at the time, thinking that this will make them want me more. But it doesn't happen. What ends up happening is that it destroys my relationships and their trust.

I simply wasn't thinking clearly anymore. I just wanted things to be like they were. He started distancing himself from me. He was calling me less and less. I would call, he wouldn't answer. I would call him at work; no answer. I knew that he still worked there… why wasn't he answering me? I even called the barber to see if he talked to him. He would tell me that he would give him the message to call me.

I remembered his basketball schedule. So, I figured I would just pop up and surprise him. Again, you know how it goes… once I come up with these great ideas, they always go bad.

I showed up at the game. He was furious. He came over to where I was sitting and said, "What are you doing here?"

I said, "I wanted to see you."

He said, "You are not thinking about what if my wife would have been here."

I apologized and said, "I just wanted to see you…to talk to you."

He said, "Please leave. I will talk to you when the game is over."

I waited in the car until the game was over. I followed him to a grocery store nearby. He got out of the car hollering and screaming. He told me we had to stop this. He said this had gone too far. He told me he was trying to work things out with his wife. He said he didn't love me; he loved her. I was heartbroken. I thought all this time that he was in love with me, only to discover that I was just something to do!

We started to argue and cause a scene. Someone in the store called the police. The police came and asked us what was going on. He told the police that I had pushed him. What a bitch! I did push him, but why would he tell the police that. So, I said he pushed me too.

The police said, "Since both of you can't be controlled, we are taking you both in."

They took both of us into custody and locked both of us up. They told me my bond was $300.

I said, "I'll ride it out." So, I didn't have to be bonded out. I stayed in jail for 21 hours. The one call I made was to my mother to tell her to get my kids. I don't know what the call was like to Floyd's wife. I couldn't imagine how he explained to his wife why he was locked up.

I felt like a complete fool. Those 21 hours I spent in jail did me a lot of good. I had time to think about all the things I had done and all the people I had caused hurt and pain. Why did I keep putting myself into these situations, knowing how the outcome was going to be? It's never good to play with fire because you will surely get burned.

•

Needless to say that was the last time I saw Floyd. He stopped coming to the barbershop and changed his number. I eventually dealt with my feelings. I realized that I was obsessed with the idea of him being my support system. His obligation was not to me; it was to his family. I never should have messed with a married man.

CHAPTER 8

ANTWAN
Mr. Big

My cousin had a card party. My aunt and I decided to go. We arrived about 9:30 PM. That night there were not a lot of people there. It was mainly my cousin's friends. Most of them I knew. There were a couple of people I didn't know. We started drinking and playing games. A couple more people showed up and we started playing Spades. My aunt and I always played partners: we were pretty good as card partners. We would 'kick ass and take names'. My cousin and her partner were winning at this time.

They were the two people who were playing together, before we sat down to play. We called winners. We were ready to kick some ass. We sat down to play the winning team, but my cousin said, "We are tired of winning. Does someone else want to play?"

A couple of her friends sat down. They said, "We're ready."

We started to trash talk: "Y'all ready to get your butts kicked? We're going to 'set' yall" ... You know... trash talk.

One guy wasn't really saying anything, while the other guy was really talking trash. He started to crack jokes and really cut it. He started in very quickly.

This guy was Antwan. He was about 6 feet tall. He had full sexy lips, a long beard that hung down the front of his chest with beads hanging from it. He also had his hair braided to the back with 8-ball beads on them. I know he sounds like a thug. But he had his own style. If I had met him on the street, I would have run the other way. He definitely wasn't a guy I would look twice at. He was chocolate, like I like them, but the braids kind of threw me off.

He was really funny. We started talking about my trip when I went to Jamaica. I told him how this Jamaican guy was following me around and wouldn't let leave me alone. He started to talk like a Jamaican. He started to sing songs and just going in on me. He had the whole place laughing. He had everyone going. If anyone knows me, they know that when I laugh, I sometimes pee on myself.

So, I said, "Please stop before I pee all over this floor."

He started cracking jokes about me peeing on myself. It was hilarious. After a while, I didn't see this guy with a long beard, with beads and braids to the back. I saw a really nice guy that had a beautiful personality. He also smelled really good.

We started drinking a little more and I started to rub on his legs. I would hit him on his shoulder when I was laughing. I was really feeling him. He checked his phone every now and then. So, me being me, I asked, "Who are you texting?"

I barely knew this man, but I said, "Damn. Who are you texting this late?" By then it was almost 1:00 AM.

He said, "I'm talking to someone about my Girl Scout cookies."

I replied, "Yeah right. You're going to get your cookies when you leave?"

He said, "Yes."

At this point, I'm thought, *"Damn. He just basically told me that he was going to fuck someone when he leaves."*

He wasn't going to get no damn Girl Scout cookies at 1:00

AM in the morning. Well, maybe he was but he was going to get some too.

The night was going well, but it was coming to an end. Everybody was clearing out. Antwan was still telling jokes. I really didn't want the night to end. We all said our 'Good-byes' and everyone left.

While riding home, my aunt and I talked about the guy that had everyone going. She said, "He was a really cool guy."

I said, "Yes. He was really charming."

I went on to say, "Did you see how I was all over him?"

She said, "Yeah! You must have really been feeling him."

I thought about him for a few days. I thought, 'Oh, man. I wish I couldn't have gotten to know him.' But eventually, he was out of my head.

My cousin decided to have a super bowl party, a couple of weeks later. I was excited to go. I was thinking I might get the chance to see him and pick up where we left off. I went to the party only hoping to see Antwan again. I mean, yeah, I wanted to have a good time, but I really wanted to see him.

When I arrived at the party it was packed. All my family was there, including a lot of my cousin's friends, too. I was looking for Mr. Antwan, but didn't really want to ask, "Hey, is Antwan coming?"

I just thought I would be patient. More people started to come. I began to think, *"Damn. Where is he?"*

His cousin came; the one he was playing cards with. So, I'm thinking, *"Cool, he's here. I can kind of pick his brain to see if he was coming."*

Before I could make it over to talk to him Antwan walked through the doors. I was so happy I was smiling inside. He came in speaking to everywhere like he was the guy everyone wanted to see. We knew that once he arrived, there would be non-stop laughter and good times.

He spoke to me and I spoke to him. Nothing else really happened because, of course, he was into the game like all the other guys. The women watched the game but we weren't as interested as the guys. We started talking about 'woman stuff' and cleaned up the kitchen.

The game was in the fourth quarter and all of a sudden he was getting ready to leave. He said 'bye' to everyone, including me. Then he left.

I thought, *"Damn, what the hell?"*

I asked his cousin, "Why did he leave so fast? I thought he was feeling me. He didn't ask for my number or anything."

His cousin said, "He had to leave."

I stated, "Oh! I guess he wasn't feeling me."

After about two weeks, my cousin called and said, "Hey, you remember that guy that was at the card party that you was rubbing on?"

I said, "Yeah: the guy that was making everyone laugh. Yeah. What about him."

She said, "He wanted to know if he could have your number?"

I immediately said, "Yes. I didn't think he was interested."

He called me the next day. He was very polite. He was different on the phone. He was all laughs at the party, but on the phone he was shy. I really don't like shy men because I'm far from that. I just don't see why anyone would be shy.

We talked about a lot of things. He told me that he had two children and that he had been single for about a year and a half. He also said that he had been together with the mother of his children, for about 10 years. He went on to say that he wasn't looking for a relationship. If he could, he wanted to work things out with his children's mother, for his kid's sake.

It wasn't just for the kids. I could tell he really loved her and if she was ready to take him back, I think he would have dropped everything to get back with her.

At the time I wasn't really looking for a relationship, but I wasn't running from one either. I enjoyed our conversations and I thought he would be a cool guy to kick it with. We talked and got to know each other for another couple of weeks.

He finally asked if I wanted to go out on a date. I was really excited. I wanted to see how we would fare, alone together. I was curious as to whether or not he would still crack jokes and just kid around all the time. I wanted to see how he would do in person. For as you know, people can be different on the phone than in person. I knew he was shy. We scheduled the date. I didn't know where we were going and that was cool. I like to be surprised.

He said he would be there to pick me up around 7:00 PM. When he pulled up, I was so nervous. I felt like I was in high school again. He got out and opened the doors for me, like a perfect gentleman. It was so nice. I got in the car as he apologized for being a little late. He said he had to go get a new rearview mirror.

I said, "Oh, yours came off?"

He answered, "No. I was playing ball with my son and the football hit a car and knocked the mirror off."

He said he didn't know who the person was that owned the car, but he left a note on the car, saying that he would replace the mirror… just give him a call. I thought that was the sweetest thing in the world. How wonderful is that. He didn't have to do that. It made me smile even more. He earned brownie points for that.

We pulled up to Dave & Buster's. I had only been there once, about five years prior. I didn't think he would take me there for a date, but I was a team player, so I was ready to kick his butt in ski ball.

First, we sat down for dinner. The conversation flowed along nicely. He was looking so sexy. He had a gap between his teeth; that's adorable. He was joking the whole time, as usual. We talked about if he would give me a kiss at the end of the date. I love to kiss and I wanted to kiss his full lips. He was blushing the whole time. I don't think he expected me to be talking about that on our first date.

He smiled and said, "When the waitress comes back with the check, I'm going to ask her if I should give you a kiss."

I started to laugh. I said, "Please, don't ask her that."

He asked, "Why not? If she says I should give you a kiss, then I will."

Once the waitress returned, he said, "Hey. Excuse me should I give her a kiss? She wants a kiss. Should I kiss her?"

She said, "Well, yes. If you want to give her a kiss, I don't see why not."

Out of nowhere he leaned in for a kiss. Right then and there, while she was standing there, we started to kiss. It was the best kiss EVER. His lips felt so good on mine. The kiss, and his lips, were so soft and gentle; so sensual… it turned me on.

I was ready to go. We didn't have to play any games. A kiss is an important part of a date. If he can't kiss then that determines whether or not there will be a second date. After that kiss, he was going to have as many dates as he wanted.

We played ski ball; he kicked my butt. We played golf; he kicked my butt. We played basketball; he kicked my butt. You would think he would let me win one game, but he didn't. It was really fun. He won a lot of tickets. I got a basketball, a little teddy bear and a big giant blue pen that said, 'Dave & Buster's'. I still have that pen today.

We headed home and I enjoyed the ride. When we arrived, he pulled up and got out to walk me to the door. We stood at the door and looked at each other. I knew I wanted another amazing kiss. He said he had a good time, and he would call me when he got home. We started kissing and next thing you know he was in my bed. I know it was a bit soon, but we couldn't resist each other.

He did his thing. It was good. He had the BIGGEST penis I have ever seen. Not only was it big, but he could go for hours. He could cum and get right back on hard. It was amazing. He said as long as I keep it up, he would stay up.

"Hercules, Hercules!" That's what I wanted to scream, at the top of the lungs. I wanted him to spend the night but he didn't stay. It wasn't a big deal. I had a good time.

We start seeing each other on a regular basis, but we were just dating. He made it very clear that he wasn't looking for a relationship. Nonetheless, you know me, I was falling hard. He was different from most guys I have met. He didn't say the mushy things like "I miss you"; "I can't wait to see you again," or "I wish you were here with me." Nothing.

One day I said, "You don't miss me."

He replied, "You want me to lie to you."

I answered, "Damn! No, I don't want you to lie, but don't be so honest."

I liked that about him. He was always honest and straight forward. Although sometimes you just want to hear something nice and comforting. Don't get me wrong; he was a big teddy bear. He was very sweet. He's just wasn't the 'lovey dovey' type. I'm really affectionate and want to kiss and hug all the time. He wouldn't push me away or say, 'get off of me'. He just didn't initiate it. He did give me the nickname "Sweet Lips". I thought that was cute. His lips were just as soft as mine.

We really didn't spend as much time together as I wanted. He got his kids every week and on all breaks. I admired how he was so involved in his kids' life, but I felt like he needed to have a balance. I guess that was not nice to say... I just wanted more of his time. His children would always wind up with most of it. His son was either seven or eight years old, and his daughter was five, I think. He talked about them, but I didn't think I would be meeting them anytime soon. He acted like he was the mother of the children; meaning he seemed more involved than the mother.

Antwan talked about her a lot in the beginning. It was almost like his feelings were still very involved. I knew he still loved her. I often felt like he was still sleeping with her. It was okay because I was still seeing other people. But at that point, I only wanted to have sex with him…. and I expected him to do the same. I knew we weren't exclusive, but I wanted us to be.

He mentioned to me that he was in the process of buying a house. Antwan wanted a house for him and his kids. He also had a sick mother. He wanted her to move with him so that he could take care of her. He was really a good guy. He said he didn't really have the money to go out on dates and do different things. I understood. So, I was willing to treat him on dates. I didn't see a problem with that. He wasn't the type of guy that I felt like would take advantage of me. I was happy to do it.

We went out on more dates and we always had a good time together. The sex was getting better and better. I didn't know how much better it could get but he was taking it to the next level. I would feel so free with him that I wanted to do everything to please him. I got the impression that he wasn't really experienced in romancing and trying to please a woman. His idea of pleasing was flipping me all over the place, in different positions and going for a long time. That was good, but some of the things that I was used to, he wasn't into.

I was used to men performing oral sex on me. That was a normal thing; something I expected every man to do. He said he did it before with his 'baby mama'. Of course, he did everything with his baby mama. He said he didn't want to do that unless he was in a relationship. I didn't like that at all and couldn't get used to that. I'm a good time and a sure thing. My sex and head game was on point! That was a struggle for me to get used to. I was turned off about that. I was really turned off about the fact he didn't even want to consider doing it. That made me feel like he wasn't into me. I know that could be a little shallow to some, but it mattered to me.

I continued to see Antwan when he wasn't busy with the kids and getting ready to move into his home. I was proud of him. He had a good job, he was buying his first home, He was a family man; he didn't run the streets. He was a perfect guy. He was what I wanted in a man.

He moved into his house. It was beautiful. I would come over and spend the night often. I got a chance to meet his mother. I know she had to think, *"There is the girl that be screaming all night upstairs in my son's room."* I hated the fact that I felt like that was how she saw me.

Things were the same with me and Antwan. His birthday was approaching and I wanted to do something special for him. I planned this really amazing dinner. We would go out. I got him some nice sneakers and I had one of my coworkers whose boyfriend's family owned a bakery, make him an 8-Ball cake. It was going to be nice. Antwan was not the guy to share his feelings. His mother had gotten really sick and he didn't even tell me. I had to find out from my cousin that she was in the hospital. She was on life support. It was a shock to me that he was going through that and he didn't feel comfortable enough or want to tell me about what happened.

I finally talked to him a day before his birthday and asked if he still wanted to go out. He was concerned about his mom so he just wanted to stay in and celebrate. I bought some food and took his gifts and cake and we had a quiet night at his house. It was more special than I imagined. He was a little quiet, but that was to be expected. He loved his gifts and was very appreciative.

A few days later he had to make the hardest decision of his life. He had to take his mother off of life support. I tried calling a couple of times. He wasn't answering. I understood that he probably didn't want to be bothered with all the arrangements he had to make, so I tried not to take it personal. He finally called. I told him I was there for him: if he needed anything, just let me know.

I asked if he wanted any company.

He said, "No. I'm okay."

He told me about the arrangements for the service. I said, "Okay. I will be there."

Then he said, "I want to tell you something that I think you should know. My children's mother is going to be there."

I said, "I know she will be there. You have kids by her and she knew your mother. So, I know she is going to be there."

He said, "No. She has been really helping me out and she is going to be up front with me. I don't want you to feel some type of way if you see her consoling me."

"Oh, okay," I replied.

I felt like he was telling me that for a reason. I felt like he wanted her to be there instead of me. Why else would he have felt like he had to make that announcement? I didn't understand. He said she has been helping him out and been there for him. When did that shit happen? His birthday was the other day. I was with him. I didn't even know he was still talking to her like that. It was a shock. I felt like I should be by his side. That really put things in a different light. I decided not to even go to the funeral. I wouldn't have caused a scene, but I just thought it was best to let him mourn or deal with his mother's death in his own way. I gave him his space to figure out things.

We continued to see each other. I felt so stupid to continue seeing him after what had happened. But I liked him… No… by that time, I loved him.

I thought it was strange that now, all of a sudden the children's mom, his ex, was not in the picture again. I was waiting for the day that she would pop back up or to find out that she never left. I didn't know what was going on. He was always very honest with me, but her just popping up when his mother died… what was that all about?

I wasn't going to just settle for us staying the way we were.

I kept telling him how I felt; letting him know that I wanted to be in a committed relationship. I couldn't take this anymore. He still didn't want to be in a relationship. He said he wasn't ready for one. But he was looking to have sex: he didn't have a problem with that. I guess if I still put out he would still take it. I decided I would tell him it's over; I'm done.

"Erika if that's what you want to do, you can," he said.

My astonished reply was, "What? You are not going to say 'No', I want to keep seeing you?"

He never said anything that made me want to keep seeing him. He wasn't mean about it. He just stood firm on what he wanted and didn't want. He never led me on. I just always felt like I could eventually change his mind. I was always looked for some type of emotion from him. He was very cold in that way. He didn't compliment me. He never said, 'you look nice', 'you smell good', 'I like your hair that way'. Nothing.

I would ask, "Bae, don't I look cute?"

Then he would answer, "Yes. You always look nice."

I responded with another question, "Well, why don't you ever tell me?"

He replied, "You don't give me time."

I said, "Shit. We have been together all day. When is it time?"

I know you are wondering why I would want to be with someone like that. I don't know… it was weird. I still wanted to be in a relationship with him. It's like I wanted to fix him and make him do and say things that made me feel special. A lot of it was I knew he still had feelings for his baby mama.

I always would say, "You just don't like me in that way."

He would say, "I do like you. I'm just not looking for what you are looking for."

I couldn't understand why he didn't want to be with someone like me. I'm fabulous. It got to the point where I was telling myself, *"I'm done. I'm finished."* But I still would call him and ask him if I could come over. Of course, he wouldn't say 'no'. So, we would always wind up back where we started.

I was just putting myself through unnecessary shit. I had basically cut off all the guys I was talking to and seeing to be committed to him when he didn't want a commitment. I figured if I had someone else to mess with and take my mind off of him, I could get over him and move on.

I started talking to a guy I was working with. He got my mind off of Antwan a little, but not really. I remember demanding him to talk to me one day. He was fed up with me talking about a relationship, so he said, "I'm getting off the phone" and hung up. He had previously told me when he shuts down, he shuts down. He didn't get mad or argue; he didn't raise his voice. He was really calm and laid back. He said when he got to that point, he wouldn't talk until he was ready. I couldn't take that. I would call and call and call and no answer. So, I decided to go down to his house and make him talk to me.

I waited until I knew he would be settled in and in bed. I got there about 11:30 PM. I knocked on the door and he answered in a gruff tone, "Who is it?"

I said, "Erika."

He asked, "Who?"

I repeated, "Erika."

He waited a minute and then opened the door. He started laughing and said, "Did you come down here to kill me?

I said, "No. I want to talk."

We did everything but talk. We had sex... amazing sex. That's what we were good at. That's where we had the most connection. I loved him so much. It wasn't just the sex for me. It was more than that. I loved him. He was the one I wanted to spend my life with. But he wasn't ready for that.

Do you know how that feels? It feels like someone is ripping your heart right out of your chest. I felt like this man was my soul mate. I felt like he was the man I wanted to grow old with, but he didn't want to be in a relationship. What do you do with that information? Not only did he not want a relationship; I hadn't met his children.

He met my children but did not really bond with my children like I would have liked. My kids were much older than his. Therefore, whoever I dated they didn't really need to meet them or bond with them. But I did want my children to like him. He hadn't met my mother. It just wasn't the ideal situation. Most women would have walked away from this long ago. But no… not me. I had to be the biggest dummy that walked the earth.

I still continued to see Antwan, even though he wasn't changing his mind. It took a lot out of me. I almost felt like I wasn't good enough for him. All the things that I liked about him were becoming the things I hated about him. I felt it was time to take a break. I just couldn't take it anymore. I got mad like I always did and told him I was done. This time I meant it.

I didn't call or see him for eight months. I was doing well and feeling good. I was seeing the guy at work. We were cool, but he had a girlfriend. So, that wasn't going to work. I never had anyone to myself and when I did, it still didn't work. But I was now dealing with it. It felt so good that I didn't even have an urge to call him.

One of my closest friend's father passed away. I went to the funeral to pay my respects. When it came time to view the body, as I was coming back to my seat, I saw this guy that looked just like Antwan. I didn't know he knew anyone in the family. My friend hadn't met Antwan, so she wouldn't have known he was there. After the funeral, I gave him a smile and walked out. I'm really big on signs. I said to myself, *"Who would have thought I would run into him at a funeral?"* I thought it was meant for us to see each other. I know it's crazy, but I called him on the phone, as I was driving away.

I said, "How did you know my friend's dad?"

"My friend had half siblings and he worked with one of her sisters," he replied.

"Small world," I said. I told him it was nice seeing him and we hung up.

A couple days went by and he called me. Our conversations were always good. It was nice to hear his voice. He seemed different. He really acted like he missed me. He even told me he did. That was a shock since he was not the emotional type. He wanted to see me, but I was not sure. I didn't want to put myself back in that space. I was doing good and getting over him. I didn't tell him anything right away, but I did say I can give it another chance.

Maybe he is looking for a relationship now. I tried to play hard to get for a while, but gave in after a short period of time. We were back to our normal routine. Not spending the time together like I would have wanted and having plenty of sex but it wasn't enough for me anymore. I tried to have another serious conversation about my needs and wants. Pleading with him that I can't do this anymore. I needed more. I wanted to be in a relationship. He has to be the most stubborn person I have ever met. I don't understand what his problem was. It didn't take all of this.

We do everything a person in a relationship does. Why doesn't he just commit to me. He tried to explain why he wasn't ready, but I think they were all excuses. He kept saying why should he get into something when he knew he was not going to be faithful. He said it had nothing to do with other women; he just was not in that mind frame. He didn't want to answer to anyone. He didn't want to comprise on anything. He just wanted to live his life and be happy for now. I said to myself, *"He just wants to fuck, with no strings attached, basically."*

My life needed a makeover. I was working on a dead-end job. I didn't like how my life was going. I wasn't happy. I needed a change. I took a trip to Dallas to visit a longtime friend. I had a week-long vacation. It was refreshing and really nice. It was different. I decided the day I left Dallas to come home, that I was moving and relocating to Dallas. My trip was in February and my lease was up in April. I didn't renew my lease.

If I didn't do this now, I would never do it. I put in my notice at the job and started making plans to move to Dallas. I set a date when I wanted to get there and I put one step forward. I didn't look back. I was scared to go to a new place with no family, but I had to go.

My children were grown and it was time. I hated leaving my family and most of all my grandbaby, Maliah. But I had to leave. I figured I had had no luck with men in St. Louis. I would find my husband in Texas. That was not the sole reason why I wanted to move. I was really unhappy with my career. Plus, I wanted to make a better life for myself; it wouldn't hurt to find a husband too.

I told Antwan. He really didn't say anything. I mean nothing I wanted to hear. He wished me the best and he hoped I would keep in touch. A part of me wanted him to say, "Don't go. Stay here; I want to be with you. I want to be your boyfriend and we can work towards marriage." That's what I wanted him to say, but you know he didn't.

A couple of days before I got ready to leave, I talked to Antwan. He had just started a new job a month before. He was busy, so I didn't even see him before I left. He didn't even make it a point to come to see me. I know he just started a new job and he was working a lot of overtime but he didn't even try. We had been dating by then for three years. Three years and I'm moving out of state and you don't even try to see me? I think about this: I wonder if he thought I was joking or kidding because I have played games and lied about things to get his attention or to get his reaction, but he didn't even try.

Again, my feelings were hurt. I always felt he didn't make an effort to make me happy or make things better. I know he didn't want a relationship, but you don't have to be in a relationship with someone to make them happy. But we did have a relationship. We had a friendship. That's a relationship. I tried so hard for us to be together. But I was the only one trying.

I packed my bags and moved to Dallas. It was a big accomplishment for me. I left with no job and no place of my own, but I was determined to succeed. I got a job after two weeks and my own apartment after two months. I was making a new life for myself. I felt free, finally.

I still talked to Antwan and would still see him whenever I visited St. Louis. He is still very special to me, but I don't expect to be in a relationship with him anymore. I blamed him for a lot of pain that I caused myself. He was always honest; he never misled me. He never promised that he was going to be with me. I had to realize maybe it wasn't me. I always thought there was something wrong with me.

He was clear on what he wanted from the beginning. I just wasn't clear on what I wanted. I kept saying I wanted a relationship but kept getting concerned about what he didn't want. He knew he didn't want a relationship. I should have known what I wanted and stood on my decision, like he did. I should have never settled for just kicking, or sex. I should have stayed firm to what I wanted, for me. Antwan is a very honest and nice guy. I saw a lot of qualities that I would want in my partner. I also saw some that I didn't like. But no one is perfect.

I have always tried to figure out what makes people the way they are. It may be the way there were raised or what they have been through. It shapes them and makes them who they are. I love a challenge and Antwan was a challenge to me. He said 'no' when I thought he should have said 'yes'. He didn't call me back when I would hang up on him. When he said he knew who he was and what he wanted, he meant that. I liked that. I thought

MEN OVER ME

I could change him, but you can't change people that are sure of themselves. He was just another piece to a puzzle I was trying to solve. When I find a puzzle, it's very hard to put it down.

CHAPTER 9

ERIKA
The Flower

My move to Dallas was what I needed. It was a chance to start a new beginning. It was my chance to make all my wrongs right. Some people may think I was running away from my problems and anything that I felt wasn't going my way. Well, everyone should know that you can't run from your problems. They always catch up with you. I've done some really terrible things to myself and to people. I take full responsibility for all my mistakes and choices.

This is no excuse, but I have always been very spoiled. My mother has always given me the best of everything. I felt very entitled and assumed everyone had to treat me that way. She made sure I never had to want or worry about anything. So, when you grow up with a mother that wants nothing but the best for you that's how you grow up being. I'm not saying any other parent doesn't want the same for their children, but my mom didn't only want this, she showed me.

My mother raised me to be independent, loving, to care for

other people and always try to help someone in need. She would be so disappointed in the things I have done. I think she would wonder what she did wrong. I think she did a wonderful job. I don't blame anyone. But I do question if I had my daddy full time in my life if things would have turned out differently. I wonder if he could have had an influence on me when I was growing up; influencing my choices and the type of men I got involved with.

I don't know if I would have been a daddy's girl. That girl who would have called her daddy for everything. That girl that valued his opinion. Could I have asked him or told him I didn't have one abortion? I had another one a year before Mikal was born. Or could I have told him I wasn't involved with only one married man? I was involved with five married men. I also told each one of their wives about the affair. I wonder if my daddy would have forgiven me? I have also talked bad to all the men I have ever dated. They have all been a 'bitch'; they 'ain't going to be shit'! I have said anything and everything that I could think of to call them… it all came out of my mouth.

I have said really horrible and hurtful things, and then wondered why I didn't have a man in my life. I wonder how my daddy would react to all the unkind things his daughter has done. I wonder if he could forgive me for all the sexual acts that I did, to think I could keep a man. All the silly, stupid things I did to find out if a married man was cheating on me. I know that sounds ridiculous. 'He's married. How can he cheat on me?' Like breaking into his apartment to find out if someone was in there with him.

Yeah, I could go on for days about all the crazy things I have done in my life. I wonder what my daddy would say to all of that. He would probably be upset and also disappointed in me. My dad did know about the second abortion. He was saddened and hurt, because in our beliefs, we don't do that. But he eventually forgave me, I think. He never talked about it again.

I'm glad I have a Daddy or Father that loves me unconditionally.

He loves me in my good times and bad times. He loves me even when I don't love myself. I have a Father that has been with me all the way. He has never left my side. He knew what I was going to do, before I did it. I always thought he was paying me back for messing with all those married men. I said this is why I don't have a husband or have a man. But my Heavenly Father is a loving God. He is not a God that will leave you or forsake you.

There is no special prayer you have to pray to earn forgiveness from God. All you have to do is ask him to forgive you, through Jesus Christ and believe that He will forgive you. I have done that for all of my sins. That's why I know that despite me having an earthly dad, I have always had a Heavenly Dad. I have had many and have put many 'Men Over Me'. I've put men before my beliefs and I have compromised me. I no longer feel like I need a man to be happy. I have to be happy with myself before I can be happy with a man. I no longer need to have sex to make them love me or want me. I'm ok just being me.

I'm changing my life for the better. I have a new song. I have a new attitude… a new mind and I'm going to make the best of it. I moved to Dallas with the help of my God. I prayed about it and I put one step forward and never looked back. He has directed my path and He was just waiting on me to believe in myself. He would do the rest. I love Him. He is the ONLY MAN I WILL EVER PUT OVER ME.

www.ingramcontent.com/pod-product-compliance
Lightning Source LLC
Chambersburg PA
CBHW071413290426
44108CB00014B/1799